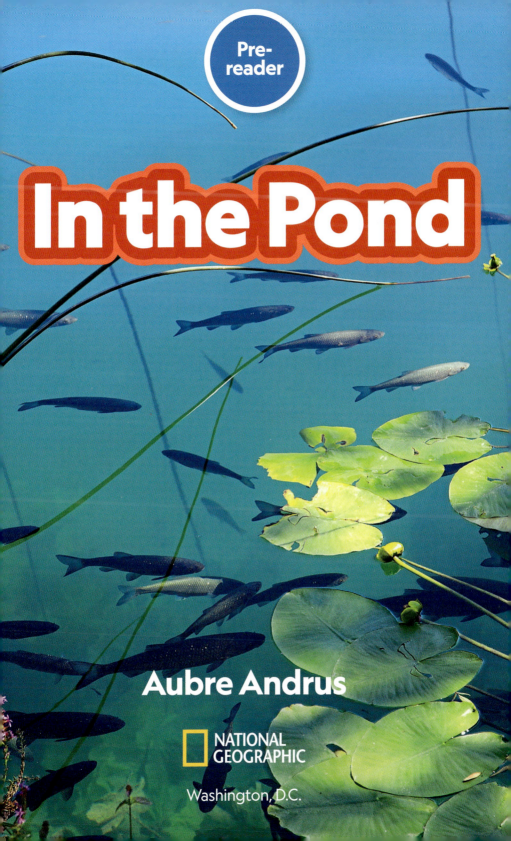

Pre-reader

In the Pond

Aubre Andrus

NATIONAL GEOGRAPHIC

Washington, D.C.

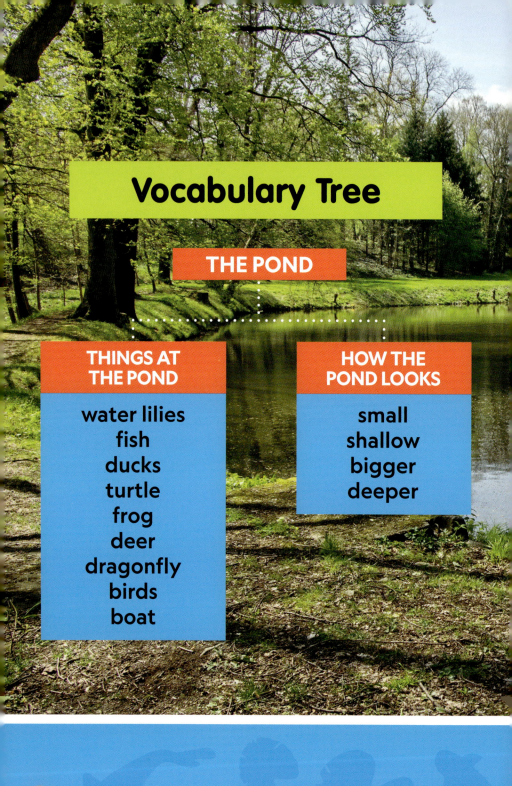

Vocabulary Tree

THE POND

THINGS AT THE POND
water lilies
fish
ducks
turtle
frog
deer
dragonfly
birds
boat

HOW THE POND LOOKS
small
shallow
bigger
deeper

A pond is water with land all around it.

Most ponds are small and shallow.

Some ponds are bigger and deeper.

This pond is full of water lilies.

The flowers and leaves float on top of the water.

The roots are under the water.

Fish swim underwater.

They look for bugs to eat.

Ducks paddle on the pond. They are good swimmers.

This duck dips its head in the water to find food.

This turtle peeks its head out of the water. It swims to a log.

The turtle warms up in the sun.

13

A frog croaks nearby.

This frog catches a fly with its sticky tongue.

More animals come to the pond.

A deer and her baby drink the water.

This dragonfly looks for a safe place to lay its eggs.

The eggs will go under the lily pad.

eggs

You can visit a pond, too. Some people like to watch the birds.

Or paddle a boat!

There is so much to see at the pond.

YOUR TURN!

What would you like to do at a pond? Point to the activities you'd like to do most if you visit one.

see the fish

watch the birds

look for turtles

paddle a boat

To Mira. Let's go see the ducks. —A. A.

Published by National Geographic Partners, LLC, Washington, DC 20036.

Copyright © 2022 National Geographic Partners, LLC. All rights reserved. Reproduction in whole or in part without written permission of the publisher is prohibited.

NATIONAL GEOGRAPHIC and Yellow Border Design are trademarks of the National Geographic Society, used under license.

Designed by Anne LeongSon

The author and publisher gratefully acknowledge the expert content review of this book by Stephen Hamilton, Ph.D., professor at Kellogg Biological Station, Michigan State University, and senior scientist at Cary Institute of Ecosystem Studies, Millbrook, New York; and the literacy review of this book by Kimberly Gillow, principal, Chelsea School District, Michigan.

Photo Credits
Cover, ijdema/Adobe Stock; 1, Janina Dierks/Adobe Stock; 2-3, Iva/Adobe Stock; 4, AlenaPaulus/Getty Images; 5, Igor Syrbu/Adobe Stock; 6-7, apimook/Adobe Stock; 7, Rostislav/Adobe Stock; 8-9, Rostislav/Adobe Stock; 10, suksamranpix/Adobe Stock; 11, Sahaidachnyi Roman/Adobe Stock; 12, Gary/Adobe Stock; 13, thier/Adobe Stock; 14, Betty4240/Getty Images; 15, F. Rauschenbach/Alamy Stock Photo; 16-17, Stan Tekiela Author/Naturalist/Wildlife Photographer/Getty Images; 18-19, imageBROKER/Adobe Stock; 19, Ian West/Alamy Stock Photo; 20, Stock Foundry Images/Alamy Stock Photo; 21, Ariel Skelley/Getty Images; 22, White_Fox/Shutterstock; 23 (UP LE), Janina Dierks/Adobe Stock; 23 (UP RT), jeanClaude/Adobe Stock; 23 (LO LE), thier/Adobe Stock; 23 (LO RT), Ariel Skelley/Getty Images; 24, traveler1116/Getty Images

Library of Congress Cataloging-in-Publication Data
Names: Andrus, Aubre, author.
Title: National geographic readers : in the pond (pre-reader) / Aubre Andrus.
Other titles: In the pond (pre-reader)
Description: Washington : National Geographic Kids, 2022. | Series: National Geographic readers | Audience: Ages 2-5 | Audience: Grades K-1 |
Identifiers: LCCN 2020005726 (print) | LCCN 2020005727 (ebook) | ISBN 9781426339257 (paperback) | ISBN 9781426339264 (library binding) | ISBN 9781426339271 (ebook) | ISBN 9781426339288 (ebook other)
Subjects: LCSH: Pond ecology--Juvenile literature. | Ponds--Juvenile literature.
Classification: LCC QH541.5.P63 A53 2022 (print) | LCC QH541.5.P63 (ebook) | DDC 577.63/6--dc23
LC record available at
   https://lccn.loc.gov/2020005726
LC ebook record available at
   https://lccn.loc.gov/2020005727

Printed in the United States of America
22/WOR/1